To Anne,
    my soul sister and friend
on her birthday, 1999.
        Love,
          Anita

Soul Weavings

Soul Weavings

A gathering of Women's Prayers

Edited by

Lyn Klug

Augsburg
MINNEAPOLIS

SOUL WEAVINGS
A Gathering of Women's Prayers

Cover and interior design by Elizabeth Boyce
Cover and interior art and lettering by Jane Mjolsness

Library of Congress Cataloging-in-Publication Data

Soul weavings : a gathering of women's prayers / edited by Lyn Klug.
    p. cm.
    Includes bibliographical references.
    ISBN 0-8066-2849-9 (alk. paper)
    1. Prayers. 2. Women—Religious life. 3. Prayer—Christianity.
I. Klug, Lyn.
BV283.W6S68   1996
242'.843—dc20
                                                                    96-6830
                                                                    CIP

The paper used in this publication meets the minimum requirements of American National Standard for Information Sciences—Permanence of Paper for Printed Library Materials, ANSI Z329.48-1984.   ∞

Manufactured in the U.S.A.   AF 9-2849

00   99   98   4   5   6   7   8   9   10

Contents

Preface

As Christians, we are part of a vast community of believers, most of whom we will never meet. Yet, through their writings, women of other times, places, and cultures can become our companions, encouraging us to take risks, helping us to go on when the way is difficult, teaching us how to pray. Through these companions of the soul God "comes to meet us in the hardest hours," "challenges us to change the world," and helps us "to behold God in everything."

Why use written prayer?

A well-written prayer is like a picture, capturing a view of one person's spiritual landscape. As with pictures, we will be drawn more to some than others. Some prayers will help us to identify how God is already present in us and in the world. Others will become a real encounter with God, transforming us and calling us to respond with our lives. Still others may reveal our longing for the relationships we would like to have with God, and with those around us. Certain prayers become favorite resting places for times when our resources are low; it is easier to accept our own struggles when we find that we are not alone.

Prayer books become like good friends, who sometimes comfort and sometimes challenge us. They connect us with "thoughts higher than our thoughts, prayers better than our prayers, and powers beyond our powers, that we may spend and be spent in the ways of love and goodness."

How to use written prayers

Prayers can simply be read for enjoyment and inspiration. Most of us have probably found those that express our thoughts so perfectly that we immediately copy them out and add them to our journal or stick them to the refrigerator door.

Written prayers can also be used as a framework or a starting place for our own prayer. We can add to them, expressing our specific concerns: What am I feeling? What work might be mine to do? What do I need? What sin or evil do I want to be free of? What do I long for? What blessings do I rejoice in? Who has forgiven me and whom have I forgiven?

Sometimes we use words because we think we "should," but if you can't honestly pray a part of some prayer, let it go. It's also prayer to be honest with God about why you can't say certain things. If you keep a journal, record your prayers along with any insights, emotions, or desires to act that seem significant. God speaks to us through our own ideas as well as through the ideas of others.

All great teachers of prayer agree that at some point we have to stop talking and start listening: "The beginning of prayer is silence . . . God speaking in the silence of the heart" (Mother Teresa).

We are not as used to this listening part of prayer as we are to speaking. One means of entering into the silence and becoming more attentive is to:

1. Read an entire prayer slowly, out loud if possible.
2. Take some deep breaths and sit quietly for a few minutes.
3. Read the prayer again. What part do you respond to most strongly? Be comfortable with silent spaces between thoughts.
4. Read the prayer once more. Be quiet. Be open to its effect on you. Where is God leading?
5. Trust that whatever you experience during this time, God's grace is at work in you.

Another way to meditate on a prayer involves even fewer words and less thinking:

1. Read the prayer slowly.
2. Choose one word or a short phrase that attracts your attention. A phrase for meditating on God as reconciler might be, "Lord, reconnect me/with my friend" (p. 47). A phrase affirming trust in God: "I will not/be overcome" (p. 111). A prayer for a church: "Come/work with us," or "Weave us/into one" (p. 71).
3. Why is this phrase meaningful? How does it relate to your life?
4. Silently repeat the phrase in rhythm with your breathing—in and out.
5. As you breathe, become aware of what God may be saying

to you. This does not always involve words. It can be an image, a feeling, an insight, a sense of God's presence, a desire to do something.

6. Be silent, resting in God's presence, focusing only on your breath as it flows in and out.
7. Close with the Lord's prayer or any other prayer you know by heart. Some of the short blessings and benedictions in this book would work well.

The many threads of prayer

The prayers in this book are gathered around seven themes of the Christian life. Prayers in "My Whole Being Shouts for Joy" express gratitude for God's immense gifts, especially for the ways in which the kingdom comes, redemption is real, and resurrection happens.

"We Are Not Alone" includes prayers about relationships—to people near and far, and to God.

Honest prayer includes questions. The prayers in "May We Always Be Seekers" help us to allow the questions in, to wonder just how God is present, to accept God as ultimately unknown, and not made in our image.

"On the Way to Goodness," prayers open us up, breaking down what is stuck and selfish. We find more and more goodness in others, and in ourselves. As our hearts are changed, our way of being in the world is changed. We do not "remove ourselves from a hard world" but "blessed, we become a blessing."

How are we to know which tasks are ours? What if we are overwhelmed by the sheer number of needs in the world? As we "Go out with Good Courage", in faith and in the company of others, we discover that "it is when we begin to do that God begins to bless."

God has promised to answer the cry of the afflicted and yet often seems silent or absent. The prayers in "How Long, O Lord?" express the loneliness, brokenness, anger, and fear that are felt by every one of us—on behalf of suffering people everywhere as well as for ourselves.

"And I Will Give You Rest" are some of the most comforting words in the Bible. The prayers in this section reveal many meanings of the word rest.

Prayers that are honest are not going to be alike. Some prayers are affirmations of hope in God and in human goodness. Others confess personal and social evil. Some are cries of despair; others are songs of joyful praise. Some prayers reflect a dependent parent-child relationship with a God who gives comfort and help. Others reflect a relationship of mutual cooperation and trust in which humans use their gifts as partners in God's work.

We know that *God* is not a male noun, and that God is neither male nor female. Because language cannot describe God's nature adequately, the use of any name is metaphorical—God is like a father, like a mother, like a light in darkness. Women for centuries have experienced and spoken of God as a gracious, loving father. Women—and men—have also experienced and described God as a nurturing mother, a midwife, a place of "unspeakable comfort". Modern women especially are seeking the feminine face of God. For others, God is more mystery, love, source, ground of being, dwelling spirit, presence. The Bible provides us with a great variety of images and metaphors for God, and the prayers in this book use many of these. As we welcome and appreciate these different images, we find our prayers and our relationship with God enriched.

My prayer is that some of these prayers will help you to discover and express truth about God and about yourself, and to live out these truths in your everyday life.

Note: If no country is given after a prayer, the writer is from the United States. If no dates are given, she is still living. For a listing of sources and first lines, please see the acknowledgements section beginning on page 149.

My Whole Being Shouts for Joy

How lovely are all the places of your dwelling, El Shaddai!
My soul faints with longing for the beauty of your presence.
My whole being shouts for joy to You, O living God!
Even the sparrow finds a home in Your presence,
and the swallow finds a place to build a nest for herself,
where she may also lay her young—on Your very altars, El Shaddai!
Blessed are all creatures who dwell in Your presence
always singing your praise!
And blessed are all the women who find their strength in You,
whose hearts are Your houses of worship.
As they go through the valley of weeping,
they turn it into a place of wellsprings.
Blessings shower on them like the spring rain.
Because they are able to see Your Holiness everywhere,
they go onward from strength to strength.
A day in your presence, O God,
is better than a thousand far from You.
I would rather serve You in small and humble ways
than live in luxury and power among the wicked.
You are a God of grace and glory, shielding and enlightening us.
You withhold nothing good from those who act justly.
El Shaddai, blessed is the woman who relies completely on You!

paraphrase of Psalm 84, Marchiene Vroon Rienstra

May you be blessed forever, Lord, for not abandoning me
when I abandoned you.
May you be blessed forever, Lord, for offering your hand of love
in my darkest, most lonely moment.
May you be blessed forever, Lord, for putting up with
such a stubborn soul as mine.
May you be blessed forever, Lord, for loving me
more than I love myself.
May you be blessed forever, Lord, for continuing to pour out
your blessings upon me, even though I respond so poorly.
May you be blessed forever, Lord, for drawing out the goodness
in all people, even including me.
May you be blessed forever, Lord, for repaying our sin
with your love.
May you be blessed forever, Lord, for being constant
and unchanging, amidst all the changes of the world.
May you be blessed forever, Lord, for your countless blessings
on me and on all your creatures.

Teresa of Avila, Spain (1515-1582)

You keep us waiting.
You the God of all time,
want us to wait for the right time in which to discover
who we are, where we must go,
who will be with us, and what we must do.
So thank you . . . for the waiting time.

You keep us looking.
You, the God of all space,
want us to look in the right and wrong places
for signs of hope,
for people who are hopeless,
for visions of a better world that will appear
among the disappointments of the world we know.
So thank you . . . for the looking time.

You keep us loving.
You, the God whose name is love,
want us to be like you—
to love the loveless and the unlovely and the unlovable;
to love without jealousy or design or threat;
and most difficult of all, to love ourselves.
So thank you . . . for the loving time.

And in all this, you keep us,
through hard questions with no easy answers;
through failing where we hoped to succeed
and making an impact when we felt we were useless;
through the patience and the dreams and the love of others;
and through Jesus Christ and his Spirit,
you keep us.
So thank you . . . for the keeping time,
and for now, and for ever. Amen.

Iona Community, Scotland

The fullness of joy is to behold God in everything.
God is the ground, the substance,
the teaching, the teacher,
the purpose, and the reward for which every soul labors.

Julian of Norwich, England (c.1342-c.1419)

Your light, dear God, surpasses all other light, because all light comes from you. Your fire surpasses all fire, because your fire alone burns without destroying. The flames of your fire reach into the soul, consuming the sin and selfishness that lie there. But far from damaging the soul, your fire sets it ablaze with love. What moved you to enlighten me with your truth? The fire of your love was the reason. You loved me so much that you could not bear to see me confused and perplexed. Can I ever repay the burning love which you have given me? No, because I have nothing of my own to give. Yet you assure me that the love which you put into my soul is repayment enough. You desire only the joy of seeing me receiving your gift. What more perfect Father could there be!

Catherine of Siena, Italy (c.1347-1380)

Magnificat

With pride and dignity I sing my song of joy
    when I feel the Lord's presence;
I am poor and very ordinary,
    but one day the Lord looked upon me
And the history of the poor will give witness to my joy.
God is unfettered and unpredictable,
    He is called our great friend.
And throughout our history He has favored those of us
    who are weak.
His triumphant force shows itself each day
    when He exposes the foolishness of the powerful.
He uncovers the feet of clay of those in power,
    and nourishes the yearning of the poor.
To those who come hungry He gives bread and wine.
And to the wealthy He exposes their selfishness
    and the emptiness of their ways.
This is God's desire: always to favor the poor.
Now finally we can walk.
He is faithful to His promises.

Chilean woman

All you clear and shimmering waters,
Praise the Lord.
All you tiny insects hovering over the water,
Praise the Lord.
All the winds in the trees,
Praise the Lord.
All you bass that avoid our lures,
Praise the Lord.
All you loons that glide and dive,
Praise the Lord.
All you chipmunks and squirrels and baby rabbits
that eat from our doorstep,
Praise the Lord.
All you huge rocks and palisades,
Praise the Lord.
All you silent canoes,
Praise the Lord.
All you early morning fishermen,
Praise the Lord.

Pat Corrick Hinton

Creator, Earth Mother, we thank you for our lives
    and this beautiful day.
Thank you for the bright sun and the rain
    we received last night.
Thank you for this circle of friends and the opportunity
    to be together.
We want to thank you especially at this time
    for the giveaway of their lives
    made by the chickens, beets, carrots, grains, and lettuce.
We thank them for giving of their lives
    so we may continue our lives through this great blessing.
Please help us honor them through how we live our lives.

Mary Fallahay, Bear Tribe Medicine Society

To the Trinity be praise!
God is music, God is life
that nurtures every creature in its kind.
Our God is the song of the angel throng
and the splendor of secret ways
hid from all humankind,
But God our life is the life of all.

Hildegard of Bingen, Germany (1098-1179)

Lord thank you for apprentice people
    who don't pretend answers before asking questions.
Thank you for enthusiastic people
    who capture ideas and run with them.
Thank you for fun people
    who carry life lightly with flags of joy.
Thank you for generous people
    who adopt unadoptables and live for others.
Thank you for unassuming people
    who don't stack their assets for display.
Thank you for deep people
    who rub against us with perspective and vision.

Jeanette Struchen

For all things bright and beautiful,
For all things dark and mysterious and lovely,
For all things green and growing and strong,
For all things weak and struggling to push life up
    through rocky earth,
For all human faces, hearts, minds, and hands
    which surround us,
And for all nonhuman minds and hearts, paws and claws,
    fins and wings,
For this Life and the life of this world,
For all that you have laid before us, O God,
We lay our thankful hearts before you. In Christ's name, Amen.

Gail A. Ricciuti

∽

Bless the small boy asleep in the front hall at twilight,
in his crumpled jacket, with a lunchbox snack beside him—
too tired to go another step, play another game,
find another acorn, or watch another bird.
This little person brought me dried weed flowers
and told me "I love you."

Judith Mattison

∽

A wandering Aramean was my mother.
In Egypt she bore slaves.
Then she called to the God of our mothers.
Sarah, Hagar, Rebeccah, Rachel, Leah.
Praise God who hears, forever.

A warrior, judge, and harlot was my mother.
God used her from time to time.
She gave what she gave, and was willing.
Rahab, Jael, Deborah, Judith, Tamar.
Praise God who takes, forever.

A Galilean virgin was my mother.
She bore our Life and Hope.
And a sword pierced her own soul, also.
Mary, blessed among women, mother of God.
Praise God who loves, forever.

A witness to Christ's rising was my mother
What angels said, she told.
The apostles thought it was an idle tale.
Mary, Mary Magdalene, Joanna, women with them.
Praise God who lives, forever.

A faithful Christian woman was my mother.
A mystic. Martyr. Saint.
May we, with her, in every generation,
Julian, Perpetua, Clare, Hilda,
Praise God who made us,
Praise God who saved us,
Praise God who keeps us all forever. Amen.

Martha Blacklock, Mother Thunder Mission, New York City

$\backsim$

My God, I praise you, I thank you for my mother.
For all that she could give me,
for all that she gave of herself,
a true, living school of love and humility.
She reveals to me your mystery—
thank you for her revelation of your truth.
Now, O God, I pray for all the children
of Africa, of Asia, of America and Europe.
For all the children of the world.
Give me a heart like that of a mother
the heart of a black woman for her children.

Mamia Woungly-Massaga, Cameroon

Through all the years of marriage,
   we've happily shared with others . . .
But God, you've given us one priceless gift
   that belongs exclusively to us,
Not to be shared with another—
   the beautiful gift of physical intimacy.
Thank you for its mystery, its wonder, its delight.
May we never mishandle it.
May we respect and cherish it always.
May our self-giving continue to be an expression of oneness,
A celebration of wholeness.
Keep it alive, fulfilling, and always full of surprises.
O God, what a marvelous expression of your own fathomless love!

   Ruth Harms Calkin

∽

Oh God, thank you for the child I carry. I am in love with it as I
am in love with my husband and my life—and you. I walk the
world in wonder. I see it through new eyes. All is changed, subtly
but singingly different. The beauty of sunlight upon the grass, the
feel of its warmth along my arms. It is cradling me in tenderness
as I shall cradle this child one day. I am mother and child in one,
new as a child myself.

   Marjorie Holmes

How good he is, my husband of so many years;
Tears come to my eyes when I see
    how crepey his neck has become,
How bravely he tries to straighten up.
Once his jaw was hard and he stood tall with no effort;
It is as if his body had been sabotaged one dark night
By some unseen enemy.
I know he feels that way.
Yet when I look at him today I feel far more tender toward him
Than ever I did when he was young and strong
    and seemingly invulnerable.
O my dear old friend-lover,
Time-ravaged fellow-traveling camouflaged boy,
Can it help you to know, can it help you to hear,
That not only as you were but as you are,
You are to me inexpressibly dear.

Elise Maclay

We thank Thee, Lord, for Memory
To live again the past;
That in remembering bygone days
The fruits of joy shall last.
But for the power to forget
We thank Thee even more:
The stings, the slights, the hurts, the wounds,
Can never hurt us more.

Margaret H. Hancock

How can our minds and bodies be
Grateful enough that we have spent
Here in this generous room, we three,
This evening of content?
Each one of us has walked through storm
And fled the wolves along the road;
But here the hearth is wide and warm,
And for this shelter and this light
Accept, O Lord, our thanks tonight.

Sara Teasdale, (1884-1933)

This morning we drove to the field (air field); excited faces around of those who had already been up. I kept saying over and over to myself, "God, let me be conscious of it! Let me be conscious of what is happening. Let me realize it and feel it vividly. Let not the consciousness of the event (as it happens so often) come to me tardily, so that I half miss the experience. Let me be conscious of it!"

Anne Morrow Lindbergh

∽

Joy is prayer—Joy is strength—Joy is love—Joy is a net of love by which you can catch souls. She gives most who gives with joy. The best way to show our gratitude to God and the people is to accept everything with joy. A joyful heart is the inevitable result of a heart burning with love. We all long for heaven where God is, but we have it in our power to be in heaven with Him right now—to be happy with Him at this very moment. But being happy with Him now means: loving as He loves, helping as He helps, giving as He gives, serving as He serves, rescuing as He rescues, being with Him for all the twenty-four hours, touching Him in His distressing disguise.

Mother Teresa, India

There is quiet at the dawning of the day,
A quiet that awaits the awakening of souls,
As all that God intends is given birth,
And Jesus is the Lord of all the garden of the earth.

There is healing in the fullness of the light,
A healing that begins in the terror of the night.
While splinters of the peace we shattered fly,
You, O wounded one, are gently putting things to right.

Did we believe the earth could be so new,
The knots untied, the torture through,
Judgment exchanged for beauteous grace?
Stand tall all prisoners of the human race!

There is victory in the coming of the Lord,
A wider, fuller peace than any soul has ever known.
What daring love is this which grants us stand
Redeemed and whole and holding the triumphant Prince's hand!
We praise our Lord's dear name with all our power!
His is the reign, this the hour!

Christine Kallman

God of joy, thank you for the gift of a good laugh.
Like music and love, it speaks all languages
and has a healing power all its own.

Help us to remember
there is nothing life-giving about being gloomy.
Let our belief in you and our trust in your care
be so complete
that our joy will be the sure sign of your presence
in this world that needs you so much.

Pat Corrick Hinton

From silly devotions
and from sour-faced saints,
good Lord, deliver us.

Teresa of Avila, Spain (1515-1582)

Lord, if this night my journey end,
I thank Thee first for many a friend,
The sturdy and unquestioned piers
That run beneath my bridge of years.

And next, for all the love I gave
The things and men this side the grave,
Wisely or not, since I can prove
There always is much good in love.

Next, for the power thou gavest me
To view the whole world mirthfully,
For laughter, paraclete of pain,
Like April suns across the rain.

Also that, being not too wise
To do things foolish in men's eyes,
I gained experience by this,
And saw life somewhat as it is.

Next, for the joy of labor done
And burdens shouldered in the sun;
Nor less, for shame of labor lost,
And meekness born of a barren boast.

For every fair and useless thing
That bids men pause from laboring
To look and find the larkspur blue
And marigolds of a different hue;

For eyes to see and ears to hear,
For tongue to speak and thews to bear,
For hands to handle, feet to go,
For life, I give Thee thanks also.

For all things merry, quaint and strange,
For sound and silence, strength, and change,
And last, for death, which only gives
Value to every thing that lives;

For these, good Lord that madest me,
I praise Thy name; since, verily,
I of my joy have had no dearth,
Though this night were my last on earth.

Dorothy Sayers, England (1893-1957)

My Lord and God,
the words of Your Spirit are laden with delights.
As often as I hear them, my soul seems to absorb them
and they enter the heart of my body like the most delicious food,
bringing unbounded joy and unspeakable comfort.
After hearing Your words, I remain both satisfied and hungry—
satisfied, for I desire nothing else;
but hungry, for I crave more of Your words.

St. Bridget, Sweden (1302-1373)

You have made me so rich, oh God, please let me share out Your
beauty with open hands. My life has become an uninterrupted
dialogue with You, oh God, one great dialogue. Sometimes when
I stand in some corner of the camp, my feet planted on Your
earth, my eyes raised toward Your Heaven, tears sometimes run
down my face, tears of deep emotion and gratitude. At night, too,
when I lie in bed and rest in You, oh God, tears of gratitude run
down my face, and that is my prayer.

Etty Hillesum died in Auschwitz on November 30, 1943.

Praise God for His mercies,
For His austere demands,
For His light
And for His darkness.

May Sarton, (1912-1995)

∽

I went to visit her,
but dreaded seeing
her body cancer-filled.
What I saw upon her bed
was a small bag of yellowed skin
full of bones.
She faced the window
away from the door I entered,
and I heard her whisper this prayer:
"Thank you, God;
I had a nice time."

Ann Weems

Magnificat

Today I look into my own heart
and all around me, and I sing the song of Mary.
My life praises the Lord my God, who is setting me free.
God has remembered me, in my humiliation and distress!
From now on, those who rejected and ignored me
will see me and call me happy,
because of the great things God is doing in my humble life.
God's name is completely different
from the other names in this world;
from one generation to another
God was on the side of the oppressed.
As on the day of the Exodus, God is stretching out a mighty arm
to scatter the oppressors with all their evil plans.

God has brought down mighty kings from their thrones
and has lifted up the despised;
and so God will do today.
God has filled the exploited with good things,
and sent the exploiters away with empty hands;
and so God will do today.
God's promise to our mothers and fathers
remains new and fresh to this day.
Therefore the hope for liberation which is burning in me
will not be extinguished.
God will remember me, here now and beyond the grave.

Zephania Kameeta, Namibia

I thank Thee, God, that I have lived
In this great world and known its many joys;
The song of the birds, the strong, sweet scent of hay
And cooling breezes in the secret dusk,
The flaming sunsets at the close of day,
Hills, and the lonely, heather-covered moors,
Music at night, and moonlight on the sea,
The beat of waves upon the rocky shore
And wild, white spray, flung high in ecstasy:
The faithful eyes of dogs, and treasured books.
The love of kin and fellowship of friends,
And all that makes life dear and beautiful.
I thank Thee, too, that there has come to me
A little sorrow and, sometimes, defeat,
A little heartache and the loneliness
That comes with parting, and the word, "Goodbye,"
Dawn breaking after dreary hours of pain,
When I discovered that night's gloom must yield
And morning light break through to me again.
Because of these and other blessings poured
Unasked upon my wondering head,
Because I know that there is yet to come
An even richer and more glorious life,
And most of all, because Thine only Son
Once sacrificed life's loveliness for me—
I thank Thee, God, that I have lived.

Elizabeth, Countess of Craven, England (1750-1828)

All praise to Him who now hath turned
My fears to joys, my sighs to song,
My tears to smiles, my sad to glad. Amen.

Anne Bradstreet, (1612-1672)

May the love of God watch over you;
may the peace of Christ fill your heart;
may the presence of the Holy Spirit fill your sleep
and speak in your dreams. Amen.

Marchiene Vroon Rienstra

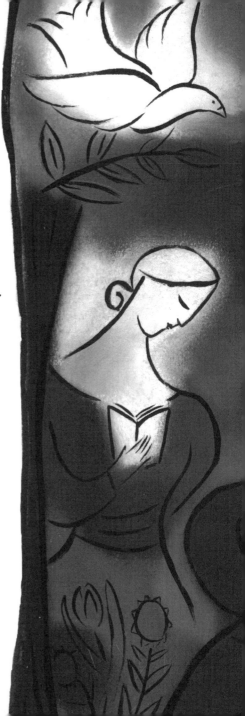

We
Are Not
Alone

Such friendships the Lord has sent us in this life. God is good. We can't thank Him enough. Thank you, thank you, Lord, for everything, but friendships especially. We are not alone.

Dorothy Day, (1897-1980)

Your love, Jesus, is an ocean with no shore to bound it. And if I plunge into it, I carry with me all the possessions I have. You know, Lord, what these possessions are—the souls you have seen fit to link with mine.

Therese of Lisieux, France (1873-1897)

Morning stretched ahead.
I longed for someone to talk to, to dispel loneliness.
I called my friend.
We talked of old times, our children, grandchildren.
Loneliness fled.
"Am I interrupting?" I asked.

"You should receive a special blessing," my friend replied.
"Before I started work I asked God to bless my interruptions."

"God is blessing me.
Thank you and good-bye."

Lord, bless my friend who listened,
who didn't make me feel like an interruption.

Catharine Brandt

O Wonderful Weaver of the World,
Help me to bridge the gap
From my separateness
To the unity of all creation.
I come as a single strand
And ask that you weave me
Into your web of creation
Together with earth and sky,
Eagle and tree,
Water and fire,
Red and black,
Yellow and brown,
Women and men,
Young and old,
Weak and strong.

Nancy Murzyn

Bless our home, Father,
that we cherish the bread before there is none,
discover each other before we leave,
and enjoy each other for what we are,
while we have time.

Hawaiian prayer

Dear God, Lover of us all, do not let me go down into the grave with old broken friendships unresolved. Give to us and to all with whom we have shared our lives and deepest selves along the Way, the courage not only to express anger when we feel let down, but your more generous love which always seeks to reconcile and so to build a more enduring love between those we have held dear as friends.

Kathy Keay, England

⌯

Living Christ, I'm in over my head. This situation is getting beyond me. Take over; take over all the way. Fill this room, this place, and all of us who are in it with your empowered presence. I give all of this to you. I thank you that you are here and that your light and love are enfolding us at this very moment. In your name, in your word, in your power. Amen.

Flora Slosson Wuellner

Lord, as once the mothers of Israel brought their children
to you that you might bless them, so now we come to you
bringing with us in our hearts those children who are especially
dear to each one of us. Kneeling in the shadow of your great
love for them, your most glorious and perfect prayer to the
Father for them, we say their names over in your presence . . .
You alone know what awaits them in life, and the special needs
of each one of them, and we humbly trust them to your never-
failing mercy and almighty love. We ask only that throughout
their lives they may do and bear what is your will for them as
perfectly as they are able, and that you will keep them close to
you now and forever.

Elizabeth Goudge, England (1900-1984)

Dear Lord, for all in pain we pray to thee;
O come and smite again thine enemy.
Give to thy servants skill to soothe and bless,
And to the tired and ill give quietness.
And, Lord, to those who know pain may not cease,
Come near, that even so they may have peace.

Amy Carmichael, India (1868-1951)

Lord, keep all my children free to love. Never let the slightest shade of suspicion shadow any heart. Help each to think the best of every other. Through all the chances and changes of life, hold all together in tender love. Let nothing quench love. Let nothing cool it. Keep every thread of the gold cord unbroken, unweakened, even unto the end. O my Lord, thou Loving One, keep my beloveds close together in thy love for ever.

Amy Carmichael, India (1868-1951)

Father almighty, help me in my special responsibility of bringing up my children alone, and look with love and understanding on all one-parent families. For the parents, help us to guide our children wisely, and prevent us from conveying to them any bitterness, resentment, or self-pity that we may feel. For the children, help them to establish close and lasting relationships without fear of rejection or loss; and in our homes grant us love, laughter, and peace.

Sylvia Jury, England

We pray, O Lord,
for all who must soon face death,
whether by illness, old age, or violence.
Strengthen them in their fear,
comfort them in their grief,
and give them some taste,
some inkling of the joy
you have prepared for them.

Sheila Cassidy, England

For all the saints who went before us
who have spoken to our hearts and touched us with your fire,
we praise you, O God.

For all the saints who live beside us
whose weaknesses and strengths are woven with our own,
we praise you, O God.

For all the saints who live beyond us
who challenge us to change the world with them,
we praise you, O God.

Janet Morley, England

You know, O God, that a very small leaf on the ground can mean that big roots are underneath. So we pray that even a little light from You, touching the earth, will mean that men and women will know of a very great love coming from You for them. We pray that this light and love will grow everywhere until everyone will have heard the story of Your way.

Nalanbana and Mijamajawui, Australia

Our Father, we pray that the church may be one in Christ, a true fellowship of the cloud of witnesses and of all those who now love and serve our Lord Jesus Christ. May the churches be conscious of their oneness in you. and speak the word of healing to this troubled world. For the sake of Jesus Christ. Amen

Sarah Chakko, Syrian Orthodox, India

Thank you, God of the lonely, for the call to wrestle with loneliness. Help me not to run from it or to give in to it by buying things, withdrawing from others or compensating by eating or drinking too much. I pray that I can be with this feeling of ache and longing for companionship and happiness. God, you have said that you will give the lonely a home. Well, I need a home so much now, a sense of belonging and of being loved, of having a home in the heart of another. Please help me to be aware of how much you love me and how strongly you are a companion to me at all times. Come, visit me with your peace and your love. Come, make your home in me and I will make mine in you. Help me to reach out to others and to go forth from here with hope in my heart.

Joyce Rupp

∽

Watch with me, Jesus, in my loneliness,
Though others say me Nay, yet Thou say Yes;
Though others pass me by, stop Thou to bless.

Christina Rossetti, (1830-1894)

I remember running over the hills
just at dawn one summer morning and,
pausing to rest in the silent woods,
saw, through an arch of trees,
the sun rise over river, hill,
and wide green meadows as I never saw it before.
Something born of the lovely hour, a happy mood,
and the unfolding aspirations of a child's soul
seemed to bring me very near to God. . . .

Louisa May Alcott, (1832-1888)

Although I have often abandoned you, O Lord, you have
never abandoned me. Your hand of love is always outstretched
towards me, even when I stubbornly look the other way. And
your gentle voice constantly calls me, even when I obstinately
refuse to listen.

Teresa of Avila, Spain (1515-1582)

God of light, hear my prayer. Listen to me and guide me in this deep darkness which is so predominant in my life. I feel as though an enemy is hounding me, trying to crush me. It presses against me until all of my world feels black and empty. You have been a source of light to me so many times in the past. I remember this with gratitude and I turn now to your light.

Joyce Rupp

Holy God, we have left undone those things
which we ought to have done,
and we have done those things
which we ought not to have done.

Yet, by thy grace, there is health in us!

In thy mystery, carry us on.
As we bring unity and joy, humble us.
As we bring division and pain, forgive us.
In our struggling, strengthen us.
In our stumbling, lift us.
When we weep, comfort us.
When we laugh, enjoy us. Amen.

Carter Heyward

I believe, although everything
hides you from my faith.
I believe, although everything shouts No! to me . . .
I believe, although everything may seem to die.
I believe, although I no longer would wish to live,
because I have founded my life
on a sincere word,
on the word of a Friend,
on the word of God.

I believe, although I feel alone in pain.
I believe, although I see people hating.
I believe, although I see children weep,
because I have learnt with certainty
that he comes to meet us
in the hardest hours,
with his love and his light.
I believe, but increase my faith.

Brazilian hymn

My soul flowers in the light of your love, my God,
and my spirit sings Alleluia in the reality of your joyful presence,
because you have chosen my kinswoman and me
with the summons of your eyes.
Yes, we are known now and for all time.
We are known as women, blessed.
Holy is your name.
The tenderness of your hand rests on us as we journey in your way.
Your power in my life has led me into the embrace of loving arms.
You have exposed my lonely pride
that I might turn my head to your nurturing breast.
You have revealed the hollowness of achievements
and have opened in my heart
a space filled with simple, loving, moments.
My hunger you have satisfied, my excess you have ignored.
You are my help as I remember your tender love for me,
. . . for we have touched each other you and I
and we have made promises. . .
I remember your tenderness for all that you have begun in me
and in those with whom I walk
and I respond with all that I am becoming,
in this hour and in all times to come.

Ann Johnson

Thank you, Lord Jesus
that you will be our hiding place,
whatever happens.

Corrie ten Boom, Holland (1892-1983)

God to enfold me,
God to surround me,
God in my speaking,
God in my thinking.

God in my sleeping,
God in my waking,
God in my watching,
God in my hoping.

Traditional Celtic

May We
Always
Be Seekers

It seems to me Lord
that we search much too desperately for answers,
when a good question holds as much grace as an answer.
Jesus,
you are the Great Questioner.
Keep our questions alive,
that we may always be seekers rather than settlers.
Guard us well from the sin of settling in
with our answers hugged to our breasts.
Make of us a wondering, far-sighted, questioning, restless people
And give us the feet of pilgrims on this journey unfinished.

Macrina Wiederkehr

O God,
who am I now?
Once, I was secure in familiar territory,
in my sense of belonging,
unquestioning of the norms of my culture,
the assumptions built into my language,
the values shared by my society.
But now you have called me out and away from home
and I do not know where you are leading.
I am empty, unsure, uncomfortable.
I have only a beckoning star to follow.
Journeying God,
pitch your tent with mine
so that I may not become deterred
by hardship, strangeness, doubt.
Show me the movement I must make
toward a wealth not dependent on possessions
toward a wisdom not based on books
toward a strength not bolstered by might
toward a God not confined to heaven
but scandalously earthed, poor, unrecognized . . .
Help me find myself
as I walk in others' shoes.

Kate Compston, England

O God,
I feel I have been sleepwalking my way through life;
Waiting in no woman's land
For something significant to happen;
For someone to come and lead me to the Real Life.
Alone, I have felt insignificant,
Unable to take control of my own life;
Not sure of what my life is.
Help me to wake up
And measure my present realities;
Who I am, where I am, and what I can be;
To kiss Sleeping Beauty goodbye once and for all
As I learn to put my trust in You.

Kathy Keay, inspired by Madonna Kolbenschlag

O God
help me to believe
the truth about myself—
no matter how beautiful it is!

Macrina Wiederkehr

O Merciful One, I come to you
As the Samaritan woman came to Jacob's well,
Seeking to quench her thirst.
Tell me who I am.
I have looked for you outside myself,
Seeking you in the streams of other lives.
In the visions of other's dreams.
Yet my thirst remains.
Tell me who I am.
Speak to me from the wells of your mercy and love.
Reveal to me my inner waters of healing and renewal.
Tell me who I am.
Release the waters of compassion and caring,
Healing and hope that flow within my body.
Let these waters flow through my life
and overflow into the lives of others.
Tell me who I am.

Nancy Murzyn

Choosing God,
Choosing to let your child be born in poverty
and of doubtful parentage
Choosing an occupied country with unstable rulers
Choosing the risk of his dying in a dirty stable
after a long journey by a pregnant teenager
Choosing to let him grow up poor, and in danger,
and misunderstood by those who loved him,
Choosing God
we doubt the wisdom of your choices then,
and we doubt them now,
while the rich are still full
and it is the poor who get sent empty away.
Help us, lest we in our anger or ignorance
choose to walk another way.

Mothers' Union, Durham, England

O God, if You are up there, out there, in here,
I yearn to say, "Give me a sign."
I've been taught not to ask for signs,
But so much of what I've been taught
Has turned out to be untrue.
I know I should have faith,
Shouldn't question,
Shouldn't doubt,
But however hard I tried,
Could I hide from You
This desperate screaming ache to ask,
Do You exist?
Will I
When I have died?

Elise Maclay

Keep my heart open to loving others and to being loved by them, God. Do not allow me to close off my life because of the scars of painful rejection. Lead me into peace of heart. Help me to believe in my own goodness, so much so that I can reach out to others with confidence and receive their affection with trust. I pray for all those who have been brutally and harshly betrayed . . . and I pray for the one who has rejected me. Jesus you continued to be a loving person even though you had been so painfully treated. Please help me to be a loving person, too. Amen.

Joyce Rupp

$\sim$

Oh, God, we go through life so lonely, needing what other people can give us, yet ashamed to show that need. And other people go through life so lonely, hungering for what it would be such a joy for us to give. Dear God, please bring us together, the people who need each other, who can help each other, and would so enjoy each other.

Marjorie Holmes

Go with the strength you have.
Go simply, lightly, gently,
in search of Love.
And the Spirit go with you.

Kiamu Cawidrone

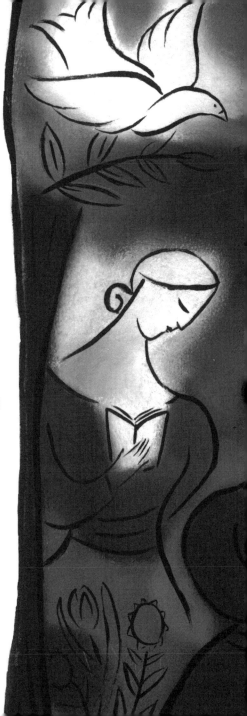

On the
way to
Goodness

Lord, on the way to goodness, when we stumble, hold us,
when we fall, lift us up, when we are hard pressed by evil,
deliver us, when we turn from what is good, turn us back, and
bring us at last to your glory.

Mary Batchelor, England

The soul is kissed by God in its innermost regions.
With interior yearning, grace and blessing are bestowed.
It is a yearning to take on God's gentle yoke,
It is a yearning to give one's self to God's Way.

The marvels of God are not brought forth from one's self.
Rather, it is more like a chord, a sound that is played.
The tone does not come out of the chord itself, but rather,
through the touch of the Musician.
I am, of course, the lyre and harp of God's kindness!

Hildegard of Bingen, Germany (1098-1179)

Spirit of love, who moves with creation,
drawing the threads to color and design,
life into life, you knit our true salvation:
Come, work with us, and weave us into one.
Though we have frayed the fabric of your making,
tearing away from all that you intend,
yet to be whole, humanity is aching:
Come, work with us, and weave us into one.
Great loom of God, where history is woven,
you are the frame that holds us to the truth,
Christ is the theme, the pattern you have given:
Come, work with us, and weave us into one.

Worship Workshop, WCC Assembly, Melbourne, 1991

We call upon the Earth, our planet home,
with its beautiful depths and soaring heights,
its vitality and abundance of life,
and together we ask that it:
Teach us and show us the way.

We call upon all those who have lived on this earth,
our ancestors and our friends,
who dreamed the best for future generations,
and upon whose lives our lives are built,
and with thanksgiving we call upon them to:
Teach us and show us the way.

We call upon all that we hold most sacred,
the presence and power of the Great Spirit of love and truth
which flows through all the universe . . .
to be with us to:
Teach us and show us the way.

Chinook blessing litany
Chinook Learning Center, Whidbey Island, Washington

In the stillness of my expectant heart let Wisdom arise, O Lord. In the midst of turmoil, conflict, and suffering, let Wisdom arise, O Lord. In joy and ecstasy, let Wisdom arise, O Lord. In the fullness of life and in each diminishment, let Wisdom arise, O Lord. As this life draws to an end and the new life approaches, let Wisdom arise, O Lord.

Spirit of Wisdom, when I am in the midst of experiencing my own sin and evil give me the Wisdom to know my own goodness. When I am inflated and identify with my goodness, blinded to my own evil and sin, give me the Wisdom to know the truth. Great Wisdom abiding in me, create me anew, bring me to my own fullness and the fullness of time. Wisdom, let me be the source of bringing others and this world of ours to your fullness of time.

Janice Brewi and Anne Brennan

∽

Holy Spirit, think through me till your ideas are my ideas.

Amy Carmichael, India (1868-1951)

Look at my fists—clenched tight!
I have been stewing all day over her conversation.
I rehash the words and what I wish I had said.
And now I have caught myself in a fit of revenge.
I have been scheming all day, haven't I?
Am I so easily bruised and so doggedly proud
        that I cannot turn the other cheek?
Have I spent one moment putting the best construction
        on her acts,
looking for a reason for her behavior?
"Vengeance is mine," says the Lord.
I had better let you take over this revenge for me, Lord,
because it is consuming all that is loving in me.
Forgive me.

Judith Mattison

May thy grace, O Lord, make that possible to me which seems
impossible to me by nature.

Amy Carmichael, India (1868-1951)

Our God, whose truth is our freedom,
we come confessing.
There are times when we talk too much.
There are times when we repeat things
which we have no right to repeat.
We pass on a story about someone that may not be entirely true,
or add our own embroidered flourish to a tale in the telling.
Forgive us these thoughtless,
sometimes deliberate,
but always destructive
betrayals of confidence.
Forgive, and help us to keep a deliberate and constant check
        on our tongues.
Keep safe within us the hurts and secrets
which were entrusted to us for safekeeping.

Jo Carr and Imogene Sorley

Mystery made manifest, One God,
Have mercy upon us.
If You give Your unsearchable riches to us,
Only to find
We happily cling
To the counterfeit treasures of this world,
Lord, be patient with us.
If You must see in us
That riches are such things as we can count,
And touch, and feel, and own,
While we must learn from You
A wealth named truth,
Inherited through pain,
Lord, be patient with us.
If you should find us small, afraid, and hidden
Behind the clutter of things we schemed to get,
Lord, be patient with us.

If we need time to turn away from wants
And know Your gifts
As we know food and bed,
Lord, be patient with us.
And if, in the turmoil of our thoughts,
We sense at last the act You have performed,
Committing Yourself to us, inviting us to bring ourselves to You,
Lord, keep us in that faith.
For in Your redeeming love
You are manifest to us,
And we, Your frail and dusty images,
Become alive to You.
Lord, have mercy on us.
Christ have mercy on us.
Lord, have mercy on us.

Kay Smallzried

Renew my will from day to day,
Blend it with Thine, and take away
All that now makes it hard to say,
"Thy will be done!"

Charlotte Elliot, (1789-1871)

How rigid and inflexible I am! I can overcome my own stubbornness only with the greatest difficulty. And yet, when I beg you for help, you seem to do nothing. Are you ignoring me on purpose? Are you waiting for me to take the thorns of sin from my flesh before you will assist me? Yes, I know I must dig out these thorns before they poison and destroy me completely. But I cannot do it without you.

Hildegard of Bingen, Germany (1098-1179)

Penetrate these murky corners where we hide memories, and tendencies on which we do not care to look, but which we will not yield up freely to you, that you may purify and transmute them. The persistent buried grudge, the half-acknowledged enmity which is still smoldering; the bitterness of that loss we have not turned into sacrifice, the private comfort we cling to, the secret fear of failure which saps our initiative and is really inverted pride; the pessimism which is an insult to your joy. Lord, we bring all these to you, and we review them with shame and penitence in your steadfast light.

Evelyn Underhill, England (1875-1941)

Creating Spirit:
Our child, so precious a creation,
lies there breathing, sleeping, dreaming his own life.
May I today give birth anew
to what needs to be created in me, released by me,
So that it, too, can have a life of its own.

Carolyn Stahl Bohler

Grandfather,
Look at our brokenness.
We know that in all creation
Only the human family has strayed from the Sacred Way.
We know that we are the ones who are divided
And we are the ones who must come back together
To walk in the Sacred Way.
Grandfather, Sacred One,
Teach us love, compassion, and honor,
That we may heal the Earth
And heal each other.

Ojibway prayer, Canada

⌇

O Source of all true wisdom and goodness, how often we substitute our own wisdom and goodness for the way of life shown to us by Jesus Christ. Forgive us, open our hearts to the simple, gentle, loving ways Jesus taught, and empower us by your Spirit so to live. Amen.

Ruth C. Duck

O Lord, I have done something wrong and I am afraid I will be found out. I am ashamed, but more than that, I am afraid that people who love me will be ashamed. O Lord, I know it is my fault that I have done this thing and it cannot be undone, but help me not to be a coward. If I ought to confess to someone, give me the courage. If I can make things better, show me how. And above all, do not let me add bad to bad because I am too afraid to let someone know what I have done.

Avery Brooke

My Lord I love you.
My God I am sorry.
My God I believe in you.
My God I trust you.
Help us to love one another as you love us.

Mother Teresa, India

O thou great Chief, light a candle in my heart, that I may see
what is therein, and sweep the rubbish from thy dwelling place.

An African schoolgirl

I come to intercession, Lord, and this is the hardest of all.
Before I begin I am filled with shame and despair;
Shame, because I, who have so much, have given so little;
Despair, because there are so many people, so many problems.
Can these thoughts I offer you really make any difference?
How can I know the feelings of those whose handicapped bodies
    make a cage without a door?
How can I understand the loneliness of the unloved
    or the mentally ill?
What compassion can I, cocooned in my soft bed, have
    of the agony of giving birth on the hard earth?
Or the bitterness of a mother having only a milkless breast
    to offer her child?
I watch the endless procession of faces on the screen,
What can they know of your love and glory?
But it is the faces of the children that always start my tears.
I want to turn away but I know that you want me to see.

Joan Pluciennik, England

O Lord Jesus Christ, whose anger was once terribly kindled against those who hurt the children, we beseech you to bring to repentance all those who through cruelty, lust, or carelessness bring the innocent to harm. We are among them, O Lord, and confess with sorrow and shame that every failure of our love in thought, word, or deed immeasurably increases the sin of the world and the unhappiness of the children. Lord, have mercy on us, increase our love and consecrate it, making it active in deed and prayer for all children in danger of body, mind, or spirit, all who are hungry or homeless through war or disaster, children of broken homes, frightened or lonely children, children who look for love and do not find it. What can we say, O Lord, what can we ask? They are the innocent sufferers for our sins, as you were in your life on earth, united to you more closely than we can understand. Lord, have mercy upon them in their suffering, and have mercy upon us in our sin.

Elizabeth Goudge, England (1900-1984)

O Lord,
remember not only the men and women of goodwill,
but also those of ill will.
But do not only remember the suffering they have inflicted on us,
remember the fruits we bought thanks to this suffering,
our comradeship, our loyalty, our humility,
the courage, the generosity,
the greatness of heart which has grown out of all this.
And when they come to judgment
let all the fruits that we have borne be their forgiveness.
    Amen. Amen. Amen.

*Written on a piece of wrapping paper near the body of a dead
child in Ravensbruck where 92,000 women and children died,
1945.*

∽

Lord, make me like crystal that your light may shine through me.

Katherine Mansfield, (1888-1923)

We are the mediocre,
we are the half givers,
we are the half lovers,
we are the savourless salt.

Break the hard crust
of complacency.
Quicken in us
the sharp grace of desire.

Caryll Houselander, England (1901-1954)

God speaks:
"I am the breeze that nurtures all things green
. . . I am the rain coming from the dew
that causes the grasses to laugh with joy of life.
. . . I am the yearning for good."

Hildegard of Bingen, Germany (1098-1179)

When man learned to fight with sticks
they soon became spears.
When he learned to fight with stones
they soon became bombs.
Now he flies the skies and sails the seas,
and all his armies march.
Lord help the leaders of mankind to realize the power
    which science puts into their hands.
Help them to learn the ways of peace before hate and ignorance
    destroy our race:
Through Jesus Christ our Lord. Amen.

Susan Heywood, England

O Lord, I don't want to be a spectator
A tour passenger looking out upon the real world,
An audience to poverty and want and homelessness.

Lord, involve me—call me—
implicate me—commit me—
Lord—help me to step off the bus.

Freda Rajotte, Canada

Why me, Lord?
Right in the middle of a strange, mixed-up world.
And with this nagging awareness within me
that you want me
to do something
or say something
or be something
that will make a difference.
It may not change the course of history—
but it may change the course of some life.
And I am obligated to respond to your call.
Why me, Lord?
I don't know why. I only know the unrest,
the divine discontent,
the eagerness on one hand to charge off in service for you,
and the agony on the other of not knowing in what direction.
Why me, Lord?
And what, *what* would you have me do?

Jo Carr and Imogene Sorley

O God, whose word is fruitless
when the mighty are not put down,
the humble remain humiliated,
the hungry are not filled and the rich are;
make good your word, and begin with us.
Open our hearts and unblock our ears
to hear the voices of the poor and share their struggle;
and send us away empty with longing
for your promises to come true
in Jesus Christ. Amen.

Janet Morley, England

෬

Grandfather, Great Spirit, you have been always, and before
you nothing has been. There is no one to pray to but you. The
star nations all over the heavens are yours, and yours are the
grasses of the earth. You are older than all need, older than all
pain and prayer. Grandfather, Great Spirit, fill us with the light.
Give us the strength to understand and the eyes to see. Teach us
to walk the soft earth as relatives to all that live. Help us, for
without you we are nothing.

Sioux prayer

Give us big hearts, dear God;
big enough to embrace all our sisters and brothers
especially those in trouble,
whether of their own making
　　or because of wrongs done to them.
Give us big hearts, dear God;
big enough to acknowledge our own weakness
　　before pointing the finger at others;
big enough to be humble when blessed with your good gifts,
　　denied to so many.
Give us big hearts, dear God;
to reach out again and again
　　to those who cannot help themselves
until hope is restored to them,
and we, thorn-beaten and bloodied
allow our loving to become more like yours.

Kathy Keay, England

The risen, living Christ
Calls me by my name;
Comes to the loneliness within me;
Heals that which is wounded in me;
Comforts that which grieves in me;
Seeks for that which is lost within me;
Releases me from that which has dominion over me;
Cleanses me of that which does not belong to me;
Renews that which feels drained within me;
Awakens that which is asleep in me;
Names that which is formless within me;
Empowers that which is newborn within me;
Consecrates and guides that which is strong within me;
Restores me to this world which needs me;
Reaches out in endless love to others through me.

Flora Slosson Wuellner

O Heart of Love, I place all my trust in You.
I fear all things from my own weakness,
but I hope for all things from Your goodness.

Marguerite-Marie Alacoque, France (1647-1690)

Signing yourself with your thumb
       on your forehead, lips, and heart, pray these words:
"May Christ be in my thoughts,
on my lips,
and in my heart.
Amen."

Gloria Durka

Go Out
with Good
Courage

O Lord God,
who has called us Your servants
to ventures of which we cannot see the ending,
by paths as yet untrodden
and through perils unknown:
Give us faith to go out with good courage,
not knowing where we go,
but only that Your hand is leading us
and Your love supporting us. Amen.

Lutheran Book of Worship, p 153

I arise, facing East,
I am asking toward the light,
I am asking that my day
Shall be beautiful with light.
I am asking that the place
Where my feet are shall be light,
That as far as I can see
I shall follow it aright.
I am asking for the courage
To go forward through the shadow,
I am asking toward the light.

Mary Austin

I want to begin this day with thankfulness, and continue it with eagerness. I shall be busy; let me set about things in the spirit of service to you and to my fellows, that Jesus knew in the carpenter's shop in Nazareth. I am glad that he drew no line between work sacred and secular. Take the skill that resides in my hands, and use it today; take the experience that life has given me, and use it; keep my eyes open, and my imagination alert, that I may see how things look to others, especially the unwell, the worried, the overworked. For your love's sake. Amen.

Rita Snowden, New Zealand

God, our Heavenly Father, we draw near to Thee with thankful hearts because of all Thy great love for us. We thank Thee most of all for the gift of Thy dear son, in whom alone we may be one. We are different one from another in race and language, in material things, in gifts, in opportunities, but each of us has a woman's heart, knowing joy and sorrow, pleasure and pain. We are one in our need of Thy forgiveness, Thy strength, Thy love; make us one in our common response to Thee, that bound by a common love and freed from selfish aims we may work for the good of all and the advancement of Thy Kingdom. Through Jesus Christ, our Lord.

Queen Salote, Tonga Islands

O God of mercy, we cannot understand . . .
        why all of our needs are provided
while others are still oppressed with need.
We could have been born in another land.
We pray for all who lack food and clothing,
who are cold and ill,
who have lost home and country,
who are disheartened and discouraged,
who are unemployed or underemployed.
Give us the will and provide the grace to love them all in you
and in loving to help bear their burdens and meet their needs.
In Christ's name, we pray. Amen.

Mildred Tengbom

Dear God, somehow many of us have grown to adulthood
believing we are not intelligent, experienced, or wise enough to
give our opinion and share our insight. We passively wait for
leaders to solve every problem. Keep us aware that each of us
has something to offer—a personal wisdom different from any-
one else's. And we can never know what influence we might
have unless we speak up in the spirit of Christian love. Give us
courage to share what you have revealed to us. Amen.

Mary Zimmer

Do not retreat into your private world,
That place of safety, sheltered from the storm,
Where you may tend your garden, seek your soul,
And rest with loved ones where the fire burns warm.

To tend a garden is a precious thing,
But dearer still the one where all may roam,
The weeds of poison, poverty, and war,
Demand your care, who call the earth your home.

To seek your soul it is a precious thing,
But you will never find it on your own,
Only among the clamor, threat, and pain
Of other people's need will love be known.

To rest with loved ones is a precious thing,
But peace of mind exacts a higher cost,
Your children will not rest and play in quiet,
While they still hear the crying of the lost.

Do not retreat into your private world,
There are more ways than firesides to keep warm;
There is no shelter from the rage of life,
So meet its eye, and dance within the storm.

Kathy Galloway, Iona Community, Scotland

Dearest Lord, may I see you today and every day in the person of your sick, and whilst nursing them minister unto you. Though you hide yourself behind the unattractive disguise of the irritable, the exacting, the unreasonable, may I still recognize you and say: "Jesus, my patient, how sweet it is to serve you." Lord, give me this seeing faith, then my work will never be monotonous. I will ever find joy in humoring the fancies and gratifying the wishes of all poor sufferers. O beloved sick, how doubly dear you are to me, when you personify Christ; and what a privilege is mine to be allowed to tend you. Sweetest Lord, make me appreciative of the dignity of my high vocation, and its many responsibilities. Never permit me to disgrace it by giving way to coldness, unkindness, or impatience. And, O God, while you are Jesus, my patient, deign also to be to me a patient Jesus, bearing with my faults, looking only to my intention, which is to love and serve you in the person of each of your sick. Lord, increase my faith, bless my efforts and work, now and for evermore.

Mother Teresa, India

It is your business and others' to go forth, confronting them face to face, for that is the only way of bringing them to Me. For when you are face to face with them, you love them, and once you love them, then I can speak through you.

Catherine de Hueck Doherty, Canada

Lord, we know that you'll be coming down the line today, so, Lord, help us to treat you well, help us to treat you well.

Mary Glover, African-American woman helping with the weekly foodline a mile and a half from the White House

It's easy, Lord, to take my parents for granted.
If I walk in blindness,
create in me the ability to see and meet their needs.
If I am deaf,
help me to hear and respond to their fears.
I thank you Lord, for enriching their lives with opportunities
to be useful, make friends, and share laughter.
If illness or aging changes them,
show me how to receive their requests with understanding—
not feeling guilty for things I cannot do.
When I was a child they held my hand;
now enable me to give my support,
and most of all, my love.

Lois Walfrid Johnson

Jesus, who never grew old, it is not easy for any of us to face
old age. It is fine to be young, attractive, strong. Old age
reminds us of weakness and dependence on others. But to be
your disciple means accepting weakness and interdependence.
Because of you we can rejoice in weakness in ourselves, and
be tender to it in others.

Monica Furlong, England

Blessed are you who take time to listen to defective speech,
  for you help us to know that if we persevere,
  we can be understood.
Blessed are you who walk with us in public places
  and ignore the stares of strangers,
  for in your companionship we find havens of relaxation.
Blessed are you that never bid us 'hurry up'
  and more blessed are you that do not snatch our tasks
  from our hands to do them for us,
  for often we need time rather than help.
Blessed are you who stand beside us as we enter new ventures,
  for our failures will be outweighed by times
  we surprise ourselves and you.
Blessed are you who ask for our help,
  for our greatest need is to be needed.
Blessed are you when by all these things you assure us
  that the thing that makes us individuals
  is not our peculiar muscles,
  nor our wounded nervous system,
  but the God-given self that no infirmity can confine.

Marjorie Chappell, England

We are going home to many who cannot read,
so, Lord, make us to be Bibles,
so that those who cannot read the Book
can read it in us.

*Chinese woman, after four months of Bible class in which
refugee women learned to read*

God of endless possibility, we confess that we do not always
perceive the opportunities you place before us. Caught up in
our own hopes, plans, and fantasies, and crushed when they
disappoint us, we are slow to see the open pathways you set
before us. Open our eyes, that we may accept the new life you
offer us, and thus show forth the resurrection of Jesus Christ.
Amen.

Ruth C. Duck

God, take me by Your hand. I shall follow You dutifully, and not resist too much. I shall evade none of the tempest life has in store for me. I shall try to face it all as best as I can . . . I shall never again assume, in my innocence, that any peace that comes my way will be eternal. I shall accept all the inevitable tumult and struggle . . . I shall follow wherever Your hand leads me and shall try not to be afraid. I shall try to spread some of my warmth, of my genuine love for others, wherever I go . . . I don't want to be anything special, I only want to try to be true to that in me which seeks to fulfill its promise.

Etty Hillesum, Holland (1914-1943)

Lord, I'm lonely, a sparrow alone on the housetop.
Yes, I know you are right here,
But I crave human companionship. Is that wrong, Lord?
Someone to sit awhile, to look at me and see me,
to listen and really hear.
Someone to say, "You count with me. I care about you."
Lord Jesus, you visited the lonely world.
You brought love and comfort to the solitary.
Turn me about. Let me reach out.
Is there someone I can listen to?
Someone in need of my companionship and your love?

Catharine Brandt

Loving God, thank you for always being ready to listen to me.
You are always there. Forgive me for being so busy that I often
forget to listen, especially to the children. It's alarming to think
that any of us could be busy doing good things, even great
things, and yet fail to listen to a child. Teach me to listen while
there's still time.

Pat Corrick Hinton

Blessed be the works of your hands, O Holy One.
Blessed be these hands that have touched life.
Blessed be these hands that have nurtured creativity.
Blessed be these hands that have held pain.
Blessed be these hands that have embraced with passion.
Blessed be these hands that have tended gardens.
Blessed be these hands that have closed in anger.
Blessed be these hands that have planted new seeds.
Blessed be these hands that have harvested ripe fields.
Blessed be these hands that have cleaned, washed,
    mopped, scrubbed.
Blessed be these hands that have become knotty with age.
Blessed be these hands that are wrinkled
    and scarred from doing justice.
Blessed be these hands that have reached out and been received.
Blessed be these hands that hold the promise of the future.
Blessed be the works of your hands, O Holy One.

Diann Neu

To be fully human, fully myself,
To accept all that I am, all that you envision,
This is my prayer.
Walk with me out to the rim of life,
Beyond security.
Take me to the exquisite edge of courage
And release me to become.

Sue Monk Kidd

God give me work
Till my life shall end
And life
Till my work is done.

on the grave of Winifred Holtby, England (1898-1935)

Lord, I search for some sense in life.
I look for some tomorrow when I shall see—and know.
And then life will begin to have pattern and meaning.
But what I have is today:
I see dimly, I know little, and life is very ordinary.
So I wait for tomorrow, dreamily, and allow my today to slip by.
Vague anticipation of fulfillment some day
    robs me of the only day that is truly mine.
Lord God, you have called me to live in the *now*;
air castles aren't for real; life is.
If this were the only day I had on earth,
    what would I do with it?
This is the only day I have right now; I dare not waste it.
Lord, keep me keenly, sharply aware
    of the immediacy of my living.
Keep me vitally awake this day. Amen.

Jo Carr and Imogene Sorley

Lord Jesus,
sometimes my life is so full,
so busy and preoccupied,
I forget there are many
for whom the days are long and lonely.
At this time in my life
it's hard to imagine
what it would be like
to be old
or neglected
or without a friend.
I know how important these older folks
are to you, Lord.
Show me how to make them feel
important and valuable,
how to let them be
at the center of my life,
not out on the fringes.
Give me the good sense
to learn from their wisdom and experience.
Bless them, Lord,
and keep them in your peace.

Pat Corrick Hinton

Hurting, they came to him.
Healed, they followed him.
Grateful, they gave to him what they had and what they were.
Blessed, they became a blessing
and went out to all the world in his name.

Those who are hurt
and healed
grateful
and blessed
still move among us
in his name.

Ann Weems

Help me, O Lord, to make a true use of all disappointments and calamities in this life, in such a way that they may unite my heart more closely with you. Cause them to separate my affections from worldly things and inspire my soul with more vigor in the pursuit of true happiness.

Susanna Wesley, England (1669-1742)

God, make me brave for life: oh, braver than this.
Let me straighten after pain, as a tree straightens after the rain,
Shining and lovely again.
God, make me brave for life; much braver than this.
As the blown grass lifts, let me rise from sorrow with quiet eyes,
Knowing Thy way is wise.
God, make me brave; life brings such blinding things.
Help me to keep my sight;
Help me to see aright
That out of dark comes light.

Violet Alleyn Storey

I know that at times I will be troubled,
I know that at times I will be belabored,
I know that at times I will be disquieted,
but I believe that I will not be overcome. Amen.

Julian of Norwich, England (c. 1342-c. 1419)

O Lord, if this I am now going through is the right road home,
then I will not murmur!

Rosalind Goforth, Missionary in China (1864-1942)

O God,
through the image of a woman crucified on the cross
I understand at last.

For over half my life I have been ashamed of the scars I bear.
These scars tell an ugly story, a common story,
about a girl who is the victim of sexual abuse.

In the warmth, peace, and sunlight of your presence
I was able to uncurl the tightly clenched fists.
For the first time I felt your suffering presence
      with me in that event.

I have known you as a vulnerable baby,
as a brother, and as a father.
Now I know you as a woman.
You were there with me
as the violated girl caught in helpless suffering.

The chains of fear no longer bind my heart and body.
A slow fire of compassion and forgiveness is kindled.
My tears fall now for man as well as woman.

You were not ashamed of your wounds.
You showed them to Thomas
    as marks of your ordeal and death.
I will no longer hide these wounds of mine.
I will bear them gracefully.
They will tell a resurrection story.

Anonymous, inspired by the figure of a woman, arms out-
stretched as if crucified, hung below the cross in a chapel in
Toronto, Canada

I accept this new day as your gift,
and I enter it now with eagerness;
I open my senses to perceive you;
I lend my energies to things of goodness and joy. Amen.

Rita Snowden, New Zealand

O Lord, when I am bewildered and the world is all noise and confusion around me and I don't know which way to go and am frightened, then be thou with me. Put thy hand on my shoulder and let thy strength invade my weakness and thy light burn the mist from my mind. Help me to step forward with faith in the way I should go.

Avery Brooke

May the God who shakes heaven and earth,
whom death could not contain,
who lives to disturb and heal us,
bless you with power to go forth
and proclaim the gospel. Amen.

Janet Morley, England

How
Long,
O Lord?

How long, God of justice, how long
before you hear the cries of your people?
How long will the poor be hungry
before they are fed?
How long will children fear death
before you hold them in your arms?
How long must the weak suffer
at the hands of their oppressors?

What keeps you from acting?
For your Name's sake we ask!
Father of the Poor. Mother of Mercy.
God of all consolation!
Your silence makes mockery of your name.
Come, God of Justice.
Too much suffering, too many deaths.
You have waited long enough!
Strike quickly in our world
and today
in our hearts.

Pat Kozak and Janet Schaffran

Look upon me, have mercy upon me, O Source of my liberation, for I am heavily burdened. The cares I carry are weighing me down. I am losing all perspective. My eyes no longer see the stars in this never-ending night. I am crippled by fear and anxiety when I think of the world we are handing on to succeeding generations. Bend down to me and lift me up to face myself with courage, to look the demonic straight in the eye and resist it with a song. Let me see to another's sorrow, share another's injustice, bear another's burdens, and in the process, lose my own. Teach me to care and not to care, bid my fear be still, and let all my insecurity lose itself in Your will. Amen.

Miriam Theresa Winter

O God, we pray this day:
for all who have a song they cannot sing,
for all who have a burden they cannot bear,
for all who live in chains they cannot break,
for all who wander homeless and cannot return,
for those who are sick and for those who tend them,
for those who wait for loved ones and wait in vain,
for those who live in hunger
and for those who will not share their bread,
for those who are misunderstood,
and for those who misunderstand,
for those who are captives and for those who are captors,
for those whose words of love are locked within their hearts
and for those who yearn to hear those words.

Have mercy upon these, O God.
Have mercy upon us all.

Ann Weems

Lord, when did we see you?
I was hungry and starving
and you were full;
Thirsty
and you were watering your garden;
With no road to follow, and without hope,
and you called the police
    and were happy that they took me prisoner;
Barefoot and with ragged clothing,
and you were saying: "I have nothing to wear,
    tomorrow I will buy something new"
Sick
and you asked: "Is it infectious?"
Prisoner,
and you said: "That is where all those of your class should be"
Lord have mercy!

Author unknown

D*aughters of Jerusalem, do not weep for me, but weep for your-selves and for your children." (Luke 23: 28)*

Jesus, you have heard our tears:
the tears women have shed in silence
because we were afraid to be heard;
the tears women have held back
thinking we deserved violence;
the tears we have not held back
but were not comforted;
the tears women have wept alone
because we would not ask to be held;
the tears women weep together
because our sisters cannot feed their children;
because our sisters live in fear;
because the earth itself is threatened.

So we weep.

Janet Morley, England

O One who soothes the savage seas
and calms the troubled waters,
protect me from the violence around me
and within me.

Deliver me from demonic forces
everywhere around me.

Protect me from avenging notions
latent deep within me.

O One who soothes the savage seas
and calms the troubled waters,
protect me from the violence around me
and within me.

Miriam Theresa Winter

What are we doing, we your people? Why are we destroying one another? We show great compassion for the unborn and yet manufacture weapons and teach our youth how to use them against the precious living. We fear one another to the point of hate so strong that we are willing to annihilate those who oppose our ideals. Will we never have the power, love, and strength to say "enough, we will no longer fight our world family for any reason"? We would rather help those who need help and try to make living the joyful experience we are sure you, our God, meant it to be for everyone. Please, dear God, show us the way to your kingdom.

Grace Losi

∽

God, how much more can I stand? Help me, Lord, help me to keep my sanity and strength. God, please take some of these interminable problems from me. Disperse them, deal with them through some other channel. Surely I have been used enough. Surely I have been pursued and caught and used enough. There is not much left. Lord, restore me. Give me strength. But, oh, release me for a little while too. Please give me a respite from these problems.

Marjorie Holmes

Lord, I'm in trouble. Time after time in the past when I have been sore pressed with affliction, you rescued me. Right now I don't doubt you are planning good for me. I just didn't know how disagreeable the journey would be. How long drawn-out, how tormenting. Dear God, you know I love you. I know you love me. You have plans for my good. Grant me patience while I wait to see how you work it out this time.

Catharine Brandt

Addiction. It's got hold of me, God, and I'm powerless to stop it. It crept up on me when I wasn't looking and became a part of my being. I thought that surely I could manage on my own. I tried this way and that but nothing worked, and I'm beaten. I need help, Jesus, yours and the help of others. Bring me through, Lord Jesus, to a new and brighter place.

Avery Brooke

God of oneness, wholeness, in hurt and pain I dream of a day when I no longer feel continual distress in my body. I cry out to you to hear me, to stretch your arms of compassion to me and to embrace me with your comfort. My being needs to be filled with your spiritual energy. I am weary with the struggle to feel well and to be in good health. It is so easy to slide into depression and self-pity, to be impatient and despondent. God of the living, hear me. Fill my empty places with hope. Fill my life with a sense of joy in spite of this ceaseless pain. Help me to fight that giant oppressor of the spirit: discouragement. Remind me often of the good people of my life and of all the blessings that are mine as I struggle with this pain which is ever present to me. I praise and thank you for being a God who never leaves me.

Joyce Rupp

∽

From moment to moment one can bear much.

Teresa of Avila, (1515-1582)

Wake up
little baby God
thousands of children
have been born
just like you
without a roof
without bread
without protection.

Chilean Christmas card

∽

O Love, no more sins! no more sins!

Catherine of Genoa, (c. 1447-1510)

When I'm down and helpless
When lies are reigning
When fear and indifference are growing
May your kingdom come.

When joy is missing
When love is missing
and unbelief is growing
May your kingdom come.

To the sick and lonely
To the imprisoned and tortured
May your kingdom come

Into the churches
Into our praying, into our singing
May your kingdom come.

Into our hearts
Into our hands, into our eyes
May your kingdom come. Soon!

Czech litany

May the God of mercy, who is well acquainted with grief,
bless us with gentle comfort and healing for our sorrows. Amen.

Marchiene Vroon Rienstra

And I
Will Give
You Rest

You, who said, "Come unto me all ye who are weary and heavy-laden and I will give you rest," I come to you now. For I am weary indeed. Mentally and physically I am bone-tired. I am all wound up, locked up tight with tension. I am too tired to eat. Too tired to think. Too tired even to sleep. I feel close to the point of exhaustion. Lord, let your healing love flow through me. I can feel it easing my tensions. Thank you. I can feel my body relaxing. Thank you. I can feel my mind begin to go calm and quiet and composed. Thank you for unwinding me, Lord, for unlocking me. I am no longer tight and frozen with tiredness, but flowing freely, softly, gently into your healing rest.

Marjorie Holmes

⌒

I'm tired, Lord, but I'll lift one foot if you'll lift the other for me.

Saidie Patterson, England

How is it, my God, that you have given me this hectic busy life when I have so little time to enjoy your presence. Throughout the day people are waiting to speak to me, and even at meals I have to continue talking to people about their needs and problems. During sleep itself I am still thinking and dreaming about the multitude of concerns that surround me. I do all this not for my own sake, but for yours. To me my present pattern of life is a torment; I only hope that for you it is truly a sacrifice of love. I know that you are constantly beside me, yet I am usually so busy that I ignore you. If you want me to remain so busy, please force me to think about and love you even in the midst of such hectic activity. If you do not want me so busy, please release me from it, showing how others can take over my responsibilities.

Teresa of Avila, Spain (1515-1582)

We seek rest where there is no rest, and therefore are uneasy.
God is the True Rest who wants to be known.
God finds pleasure in being our true resting place.
God is everything that is good,
and the goodness that everything possesses is God.
God wants us to allow ourselves to see God continually.
For God wants to be seen and wants to be sought.
God wants to be awaited and wants to be trusted.

Julian of Norwich, England (c. 1342-c. 1419)

Dear God, it is so hard for us not to be anxious,
we worry about work and money,
about food and health,
about weather and crops,
about war and politics,
about loving and being loved.
Show us how perfect love casts out fear.

Monica Furlong, England

The Lord is here.
Let us in the stillness of our hearts pray
    that we may have the consciousness of His presence
    and listen to His voice.
Let us in the stillness of our hearts pray
    that God will reveal to us the things that hinder our peace.
Let us in the stillness of our hearts pray
    that we may be filled with the Holy Spirit,
    and empowered to witness fearlessly against evil.
Let us in the stillness of our hearts pray
    to be conscious of what it means
    when we say "Thy Kingdom come!"

    Michi Kawai, Japan

How should I fear to die?
Have I not seen
The color of a small butterfly,
The silver sheen
Of breaking waves and a wood-dove's wings?
Have I not marked the coat
Of mouse and deer,
The shape of flowers, the thrush's specked throat—
And shall I fear
To fall into the hands that made these things?

Teresa Hooley, England

ᔐ

God is not only fatherly,
God is also mother
who lifts her loved child
from the ground to her knee.
The Trinity is like a mother's cloak
wherein the child finds a home
and lays its head on the maternal breast.

Mechtild of Magdeburg, Germany (c. 1210-1294)

I am alone in the dark, and I am thinking
what darkness would be mine if I could see
the ruin I wrought in every place I wandered
and if I could not be aware of One who follows after me.
Whom do I love, O God, when I love Thee?
The great Undoer who has torn apart
the walls I built against a human heart,
the Mender who has sewn together the hedges
through which I broke when I went seeking ill,
the Love who follows and forgives me still.
Fumbler and fool that I am, with things around me
of fragile make like souls, how I am blessed
to hear behind me footsteps of a Savior!
I sing to the east; I sing to the west:
God is my repairer of fences, turning my paths into rest.

Jessica Powers, (1905-1988)

Oh, Lord, who on Maundy Thursday didst say to Thy disciples, "This is my body, broken for you," permit us to use this occasion to offer Thee all *our* broken parts. We ask Thee to take our broken friendships, our broken dreams, our broken promises, promises we made both to others and to ourselves; take the broken bodies of some of us, and the broken hearts of all of us. And take unto Thee everything about us which we may not know is broken, or is going to be broken, and make all things whole again in Thyself. Amen.

Gail Godwin

Lord, for the ways in which you've graced my life this week, I give you thanks and praise. I especially thank you for growing my garden and my life. Give me the strength and wisdom to be faithful in tending both my outer and inner gardens. Keep me from doing your job, from trying to force growth to meet my private timetable. I offer up to you my need for quick results and my obsession with self-measurement. Help me to be gentle and patient with myself and my garden. For I pray in Jesus' name. Amen.

Harriet Crosby

The fruit and purpose of prayer is to be one with and like God
    in all things.
It is the will of God that our prayer and our trust be large.

We must truly know that our God is the ground
from which our prayer sprouts
and that it is a gift given out of love.
Otherwise, we waste our time and pain ourselves.

When we think that our prayers have not been answered,
we should not become depressed over it.
I am certain that God is telling us that we must wait
    for a better time, more grace,
        or that a better gift will be given to us.

God is being, and wants us to sit, dwell, and ground ourselves
    in this knowledge,
while at the same time realizing that we are noble, excellent,
assessed as precious and valuable,
    and have been given creation for our enjoyment
    because we are loved!

Julian of Norwich, England (c.1342-c. 1419)

Lord, teach us how to pray. There's a busy part of us that urges us to be always out doing something. But you've told us that being quiet with you is essential too. How can we know what you want us to do if we don't take time out to listen to you? Help us not to be afraid of what we might learn if we are still. Let our lives be a work of peace because we have discovered you and ourselves in you.

Pat Corrick Hinton

Dear Lord, please give me . . .
A few friends who understand me and yet remain my friends,
A work to do which has real value,
    without which the world would feel the poorer . . .
A mind unafraid to travel even though the trail be not blazed,
An understanding heart . . .
A sense of humor,
Time for quiet, silent meditation,
A feeling of the presence of God,
And the patience to wait for the coming of these things,
with the wisdom to know them when they come.

W.R. Hunt

We all bleed.
we bleed for ourselves—
we each have our private pain;
we bleed for others;
and we bleed for a wounded world.
If we did not bleed for others
in some measure,
would we not be spiritually barren?
unfit for our calling,
incapable of conceiving and nurturing new life,
forming relationships and caring communities?
But if the pain takes over
and the bleeding becomes constant
do we not then find that
we have lost touch with our Lord?
He is obscured by the crowd of our concerns,
the crowd of our activities,
the crowd of our own words.
Jesus, help us to touch you now,
to lay before you
our own and the world's pain.
Help us, as we wait in silence
to feel your healing hands upon us.

Consultation of Methodist women ministers, Oxford, 1984

El Shaddai, I want to avoid arrogance.
I do not want to walk in ways too difficult for me,
or try to understand things beyond my grasp.
I calm myself now and sit quietly in Your embrace,
like a weaned child at its mother's breast,
my soul like a tranquil little one.
With Your people, I hope in You, now and forevermore.

paraphrase of Psalm 131, Marchiene Vroon Rienstra

Thou hast called me—I cannot tell why.
Thou wilt justify me—I cannot tell how.
Thou wilt glorify me—I cannot tell when.

Amy Carmichael, India (1867-1951)

And so our good Lord answered to all the questions and doubts which I could raise, saying most comfortingly: I may make all things well, and I can make all things well, and I shall make all things well, and I will make all things well; and you will see yourself that every kind of thing will be well . . . And in these . . . words God wishes us to be enclosed in rest and in peace.

Julian of Norwich, England (c.1342-c.1419)

May the God who listens to our hearts and enters into our pain bless us and all who are in need with the comfort and quiet of Her gentle presence, now and always. Amen.

Marchiene Vroon Rienstra

May the blessing of light be on you,
light without and light within.
May the blessed sunlight shine upon you
and warm your heart
till it glows like a great fire
and strangers may warm themselves
as well as friends.

And may the light shine out of the eyes of you,
like a candle set in the window of a house,
bidding the wanderer to come in
out of the storm.

May the blessing of rain be on you;
the soft sweet rain.
May it fall upon your spirit
so that little flowers may spring up
and shed their sweetness on the air.

And may the blessing of the great rains be on you,
to beat upon your spirit and wash it fair and clean;
and leave there many a shining pool
where the blue of heaven shines,
and sometimes a star.

May the blessing of the earth be on you,
the great round earth;
may you ever have a kindly greeting for people
as you're going along the roads.

And now may the Lord bless you,
and bless you kindly. Amen.

Irish blessing

Night and Your stars
Spread out over me,
The air cold and clear,
The smell of woodsmoke.
Somewhere people are sitting around a fire,
And I am out here alone.
Once I'd have worried that idea like
A dog with a bone,
Till I was overcome with sadness.
Now so many waves of yearning have already washed over me,
I'm unmoved,
I have suffered so many losses,
There are few to fear.
So many matters I used to agonize over
Don't matter anymore—
Getting ahead, being invited,
Fitting in, winning.
It's too late for all that now,
Too late to do much more
Than be out here under the stars
Talking to You,
Friendly and peaceful.

Elise Maclay

Deep peace, pure white of the moon to you.
Deep peace, pure green of the grass to you.
Deep peace, pure brown of the earth to you.
Deep peace, pure grey of the dew to you.
Deep peace, pure blue of the sky to you.
Deep peace, of the running wave to you.
Deep peace, of the flowing air to you.
Deep peace, of the quiet earth to you.
Deep peace, of the shining stars to you.
Deep peace, of the Son of Peace to you.

Fiona Macleod, Ireland (1855-1905)

Acknowledgements

The editor gratefully acknowledges the following sources for their contributions to this collection. Any omissions are unintentional and will be corrected upon future printings.

My Whole Being Shouts for Joy

Page 16: "How Lovely are all the places," from *Swallow's Nest: A Feminine Reading of the Psalms* by Marchiene Vroon Rienstra. Copyright © 1992 William B. Eerdmans Publishing Co. Used by permission.

Page 17: "May you be blessed forever, Lord," by Teresa of Avila, (1515-1582).

Pages 18-19: "You keep us waiting" from *Iona Community Worship Book.* Copyright © 1988 The Iona Community, Scotland. Used by permission of GIA Publications, Inc., Chicago, IL, exclusive agent. All rights reserved.

Page 20: "The fullness of joy is to behold God" from *Meditations with Julian of Norwich* by Brendan Doyle. Copyright © 1983 Bear & Co., Santa Fe, NM. Used by permission.

Page 20: "Your light, dear God, surpasses all other light" from *Catherine of Siena: The Dialogue* by Suzanne Noffke, O.P. Copyright © 1980 Missionary Society of St. Paul the Apostle in the State of New York. Used by permission of Paulist Press.

Page 21: "Magnificat/With pride and dignity I sing my song," by a Chilean woman. Source unknown.

Page 22: "All you clear and shimmering waters" from *Prayers for Growing and Other Pains* by Pat Corrick Hinton, (New York: HarperCollins, 1972). Used by permission of Pat Corrick Hinton.

Page 23: "Creator, Earth Mother" by Mary Fallahay of the Bear Tribe Medicine Society, Spokane, WA.

Page 24: "To the Trinity be praise!" from *St. Hildegard of Bingen: Symphonia: A Critical Edition of the 'Symphonia armonie celestium revelationum.'* Edited and translated by Barbara Newman. Copyright © 1989 Cornell University. Used by permission.

Page 24: "Lord thank you for apprentice people" from *Prayers to Pray Without Really Trying* by Jeanette Struchen. Copyright © 1967 Jeanette Struchen. Used by permission of HarperCollins Publishers, Inc.

Page 25: "For all things bright and beautiful," from *Birthings and Blessings: Liberating Worship Services for the Inclusive Church* by Rosemary Catalano Mitchell and Gail Anderson Ricciuti. Copyright © 1991 Rosemary Catalano Mitchell and Gail Anderson Ricciuti. Used with permission of The Crossroad Publishing Co., New York.

Page 25: "Bless the small boy asleep" by Judith Mattison, Copyright © Judith Mattison. Used by permission in honor of her son, Michael Mattison.

Pages 26-27: "A wandering Aramean was my mother," by Martha Blacklock, Mother Thunder Mission.

Page 27: "My God, I praise you, I thank you for my mother," by Mamia Woungly-Massaga, (Lausanne, Switzerland: Editions du Soc, 1980).

Page 28: "Through all the years of marriage" from *Lord, I Keep Running Back to You* by Ruth Harms Calkin. Copyright © 1979 Ruth Harms Calkin, Pomona, CA 91768. Used by permission.

Page 28: "Oh, God, thank you for the child I carry" from *I've Got to Talk to Somebody God* by Marjorie Holmes. Copyright © 1968, 1969 Marjorie Holmes Mighell. Used by permission of Doubleday, a division of Bantam Doubleday Dell Publishing Group, Inc.

Page 29: "How good he is, my husband of so many years" from *Green Winter: Celebrations of Old Age* by Elise Maclay. Copyright © 1977, 1990 Elise Maclay. Used by permission of Henry Holt and Company, Inc.

Page 30: "We thank Thee, Lord, for Memory" by Margaret H. Hancock from *Uncommon Prayer* by Kenneth Swanson. Copyright © 1987 Kenneth Swanson. Used by permission of Ballantine Books, a Division of Random House, Inc.

Page 30: "How can our minds and bodies be grateful" from *The Collected Poems of Sara Teasdale* by Sara Teasdale. Copyright © 1933 by Macmillan Publishing Co., Renewed 1961 by Guaranty Trust Company of New York, Executor. Used by permission of Simon & Schuster.

Page 31: "This morning, we drove to the field" from the journals of Anne Morrow Lindbergh, (1906-1955).

Page 31: "Joy is prayer" from *A Gift for God* by Mother Teresa. Copyright © 1975 by Mother Teresa Minnsionaries of Charity. Used by permission of HarperCollins Publishers, Inc.

Page 32: "There is quiet at the dawning of the day" by Christine Kallman commissioned for the Luther College, Decorah, IA, 1995 Yuletide Fest. Copyright © 1995 Christine Kallman, Northfield, MN. Used by permission.

Page 33: "God of joy, thank you for the gift" from *Images of Peace* by Pat Corrick Hinton. (New York: HarperCollins, 1984). Used by permission of Pat Corrick Hinton.

Page 33: "From silly devotions" by Teresa of Avila. (1515-1582).

Pages 34-35: "Lord, if this night my journey end" from *Opus 1 (1916)* by Dorothy Sayers (1893-1957).

Page 36: "My Lord and God, the words of Your Spirit" from *Swallow's Nest* by Marchiene Vroon Rienstra. Copyright © 1992 Wm. B. Eerdmans Publishing Co. Used by permission.

Page 36: "You have made me so rich" from *An Interrupted Life: The Diaries of Etty Hillesum 1941-1943* by Etty Hillesum, translated by Arno Pomerans. English translation copyright © 1983 by Jonathon Cape Ltd. Used by permission of Pantheon Books, a division of Random House, Inc.

Page 37: "Praise God for His mercies" taken from "Gestalt at Sixty" from *A Durable Fire: New Poems by May Sarton*. Copyright © 1972 by May Sarton. Used by permission of W.W. Norton & Company, Inc.

Page 37: "I went to visit her" from *Kneeling in Jerusalem*. Copyright © 1992 Ann Weems. Used by permission of Westminster John Knox Press.

Pages 38-39: "Magnificat/Today I look into my own heart" by Zephania Kameeta from *Why O Lord? Psalms and Sermons from Namibia*. Copyright © 1986 WCC Publications, World Council of Churches, Geneva, Switzerland. Used by permission.

Page 40: "I thank Thee, God, that I have lived" by Elizabeth, Countess of Craven, England (1750-1828).

Page 41: "All praise to Him who now hath turned" by Anne Bradstreet (1612-1672).

Page 41: "May the love of God watch over you" from *Swallow's Nest* by Marchiene Vroon Rienstra. Copyright © 1992 Wm. B. Eerdmans Publishing Co. Used by permission.

We Are Not Alone

Page 44: "Such friendships the Lord has sent us" by Dorothy Day from *The Catholic Worker*, December 1980 edition. Used by permission.

Page 44: "Your love, Jesus, is an ocean" by Therese of Lisieux (1873-1897).

Page 45: "Morning stretched ahead" from *Still Time to Sing* by Catharine Brandt (Minneapolis: Augsburg, 1980). Used by permission of Catharine Brandt.

Page 54: "Holy God, we have left undone those things" from *A Priest Forever* by Carter Heyward. Copyright © 1976 Carter Heyward. (New York: HarperCollins) Used by permission of the author.

Page 55: "I believe, although everything hides you from my faith." Brazilian hymn from *Livros de Cantos*, Porte Alegre, Brazil, 1977.

Page 56: "My soul flowers in the light" from *Miryam of Nazareth: Woman of Strength and Wisdom* by Ann Johnson. Copyright © 1984 Ave Maria Press. Used by permission.

Page 57: "Thank you, Lord Jesus that you will be our hiding place" from *Each New Day With Corrie ten Boom* by Corrie ten Boom. Copyright © 1977 Fleming H. Revell Company, a division of Baker Book House, Grand Rapids, MI. Used by permission.

Page 57: "God to enfold me," Traditional Celtic.

May We Always Be Seekers

Page 60: "It seems to me Lord that we search" from *Seasons of Your Heart: Prayers and Reflections* by Macrina Wiederkehr. Copyright © 1991 Macrina Wiederkehr. Used by permission of HarperCollins Publishers, Inc.

Page 61: "O God, who am I now?" by Kate Compston, England. Used by permission.

Page 62: "O God, I feel I have been sleepwalking" from *Laughter, Silence and Shouting* by Kathy Keay. Copyright © 1994 HarperCollins Publishers, Inc. Used by permission.

Page 62: "O God help me to believe the truth" from *Seasons of Your Heart: Prayers and Reflections* by Macrina Wiederkeher. Copyright © 1991 Macrina Wiederkehr. Used by permission of HarperCollins, Inc.

Page 63: "O Merciful One, I come to you" by Nancy Murzyn, New Brighton, MN. Used by permission.

Page 64: "Choosing God," Source unknown.

Page 65: "O God, if You are up there" from *Green Winter: Celebrations of Old Age* by Elise Maclay. Copyright © 1977, 1990 Elise Maclay. Used by permission of Henry Holt and Company, Inc.

Page 66: "Keep my heart open to loving others" from *Praying Our Goodbyes* by Joyce Rupp. Copyright © Ave Maria Press, Notre Dame, IN 46556. Used by permission.

Page 66: "Oh, God, we go through life so lonely" from *I've Got to Talk to Somebody God* by Marjorie Holmes. Copyright © 1968, 1969 Marjorie Holmes Mighell. Used by permisison of Doubleday, a division of Bantam Doubleday Dell Publishing Group, Inc.

Page 67: "Go with the strength you have" from *In Spirit and In Truth*. Copyright © 1991 The Iona Community, Scotland. Used by permission of GIA Publications, Inc., Chicago, IL, exclusive agent. All rights reserved.

On the Way to Goodness

Page 81: "O Lord, I have done something wrong" from *Youth Talks With God* by Avery Brooke. (New York: Scribner, 1959). Used by permission of Avery Brooke.

Page 81: "My Lord I love you" by Mother Teresa from *Words To Love By.* Copyright © 1983 Ave Maria Press, Notre Dame, IN. Used by permission.

Page 82: "O thou great Chief, light a candle in my heart," Source unknown.

Page 82: "I come to intercession, Lord" from *She Prays: A Collection of Prayers and Poems for International Women's Day, 1975,* edited by Phoebe Willetts. Used by permission.

Page 83: "O Lord Jesus Christ, whose anger was once terribly kindled" from *A Diary of Prayer* by Elizabeth Goudge (New York: Coward-McCann, Inc., 1966). Used by permission of Harold Ober Associates.

Page 84: "O Lord, remember not only the men and women," by a Holocaust victim, found on a piece of paper in Ravensbrook, 1945.

Page 84: "Lord, make me like crystal" by Katherine Mansfield. (1888-1923) Source unknown.

Page 85: "We are the mediocre" by Caryll Houselander. Abridged and reprinted by permission of Sheed & Ward, 115 E. Armour Blvd., Kansas City, MO 64111.

Page 85: "God speaks: I am the breeze" from *Meditations with Hildegard of Bingen* by Gabriele Uhlien. Copyright © 1982 Bear & Co., Santa Fe, NM. Used by permission.

Page 86: "When man learned to fight with sticks" based on a prayer by Susan Heywood. Source unknown.

Page 86: "O Lord, I don't want to be a spectator" by Freda Rajotte, Canada from *With All God's People: The New Ecumenical Prayer Cycle.* Copyright © 1989 WCC Publications, World Council of Churches, Geneva, Switzerland. Used by permission.

Page 87: "Why me, Lord?" adapted from *Bless This Mess and Other Prayers* by Jo Carr and Imogene Sorley. Copyright © 1969 Abingdon Press. Used by permission.

Page 88: "O God, whose word is fruitless when the mighty" by Janet Morley from *Tell Out My Soul.* Copyright © 1990 Christian Aid, PO Box 100, London SE1 7RT. Used by permission.

Page 88: "Grandfather, Great Spirit, you have been always" (Sioux Indian Prayer) from *Your Prayers and Mine,* edited by Elizabeth Yates. Copyright © 1954 Elizabeth Yates McGreal and Nora S. Unwin. Copyright © renewed 1982 Elizabeth Yates McGreal. Used by permission of Houghton Mifflin Company. All rights reserved.

Page 89: "Give us big hearts" from *Laughter, Silence and Shouting* by Kathy Keay. Copyright © 1994 HarperCollins Publishers, Ltd., London. Used by permission.

Page 90: "The risen, living Christ" from *Prayer, Fear, and Our Powers.* Copyright © 1989 Flora Slosson Wuellner. Used by permission of Upper Room Books.

Page 91: "O Heart of love, I place all my trust in You." by Marguerite-Marie Alacoque, France. (1647-1690).

Page 91: "Signing yourself with your thumb" from *Praying with Hildegard of Bingen* by Gloria Durka. Copyright 1991 St. Mary's Press, Winona, MN. Used by permission.

Go Out with Good Courage

Page 94: "O Lord God, who has called us Your servants" from *Lutheran Book of Worship*, copyright © 1978. Used by permission of Augsburg Fortress.

Page 94: "I arise, facing East" from *Snowy Earth Comes Gliding* edited by Evelyn Easton. Copyright © 1974 Draco Foundation, The Bear Tribe Medicine Society.

Page 95: "I want to begin the day with thankfulness" from *A Woman's Book of Prayers* by Rita F. Snowden. (Yew York: Association Press, 1968).

Page 95: "God, our Heavenly Father, we draw near" by Kiamu Cawidrone from *In Spirit and In Truth*. Copyright © 1991 The Iona Community, Scotland. Used by permission of GIA Publications, Inc., Chicago, IL, exclusive agent. All rights reserved.

Page 96: "O God of mercy, we cannot understand" from *Mealtime Prayers* by Mildred Tengbom. (Minneapolis: Augsburg Publishing House, 1985). Used by permission of Mildred Tengbom.

Page 96: "Dear God, somehow many of us have grown" from *Sister Images* by Mary Zimmer. Copyright © 1993 Abingdon Press. Used by permission.

Page 97: "Do not retreat into your private world" by Kathy Galloway. Copyright © The Iona Community, Scotland. Used by permission of GIA Publications, Inc., Chicago, IL, exclusive agent. All rights reserved.

Page 98: "Dearest Lord, may I see you today" by Mother Teresa from *Morning, Noon and Night* edited by Rev. John Carden. Used by permission of the Church Mission Society, London.

Page 99: "It is your business and others' to go forth" from *Molchanie* by Catherine de Hueck Doherty. (New York: Crossroad Publishing Co., 1982).

Page 99: "Lord, we know that you'll be coming down" by Mary Glover from *The Rise of the Christian Conscience* by Jim Wallis. Used by permission of Jim Wallis.

Page 100: "It's easy, Lord, to take my parents for granted" from *Songs for Silent Moments* by Lois Walfrid Johnson (Minneapolis: Augsburg Publishing House, 1980). Used by permission of Lois Walfrid Johnson.

Page 100: "Jesus, who never grew old" by Monica Furlong. Used by permission.

Page 101: "Blessed are you who take time to listen" by Marjorie Chappell from *Laughter,*

Page 111: "O Lord, if this I am now going through" by Rosalind Goforth. (1864-1942).

Pages 112-113: "O God, through the image of a woman" from *No Longer Strangers: A Resource for Women and Worship*. Copyright © 1983 WCC Publications, World Council of Churches, Geneva, Switzerland. Used by permission.

Page 114: "I accept this new day as your gift" by Rita Snowden. Source unknown.

Page 114: "O Lord, when I am bewildered" from *Youth Talks With God* by Avery Brooke. (New York: Scribner, 1959). Used by permission of Avery Brooke.

Page 115: "May the God who shakes heaven and earth" from *All Desires Known* by Janet Morley. Copyright © 1988, 1992 Janet Morley. Used by permission of Morehouse Publishing, Harrisburg, PA. New expanded edition co-published with SPCK, London, 1992.

How Long, O Lord?

Page 118: "How long, God of justice" from *More Than Words: Prayer and Ritual for Inclusive Communities*. A Meyer-Stone Book by Janet Schaffran, CDP, and Pat Kozak, CSJ. First ed. copyright © 1986, second revised ed. copyright © 1988 Pat Kozak and Janet Schaffran. Used by permission of The Crossroad Publishing Company, New York.

Page 119: "Look upon me, have mercy upon me" from *WomanWord: A Feminist Lectionary and Psalter: Women of the New Testament* by Miriam Therese Winter. Copyright © 1990 Medical Mission Sisters. Used by permission of The Crossroad Publishing Company, New York and the UK and Commonwealth publishers, HarperCollins, Melbourne, Australia.

Page 120: "O God, we pray this day" from *Kneeling in Jerusalem*. Copyright © 1992 Ann Weems. Used by permission of Westminster John Knox Press.

Page 121: "Lord, when did we see you?," author unknown, from *Rapidas*—the magazine of the Movement for Latin American Evangelical Unity, Lima, Peru. English translation by WCC Publications, World Council of Churches, Geneva, Switzerland.

Page 122: "Jesus, you have heard our tears" by Janet Morley from *Bread of Tomorrow*. Copyright © Christian Aid, PO Box 100, London SE1 7RT. Used by permission.

Page 123: "O One who soothes the savage seas" from *WomanWisdom: A Feminist Lectionary and Psalter: Women of the Hebrew Scriptures, Part 1* by Miriam Therese Winter. Copyright © 1991 Medical Mission Sisters. Used by permission of The Crossroad Publishing Company, New York and the UK and Commonwealth publishers, Harpercollins, Melbourne, Australia.

Page 124: "What are we doing, we your people?" by Grace Losi from *Woman Pray* edited by Karen L. Roller. Copyright © Pilgrim Press, Cleveland, OH. Used by permission.

Page 124: "God, how much more can I stand?" from *I've Got to Talk to Somebody God* by Marjorie Holmes. Copyright © 1968, 1969 Marjorie Holmes Mighell. Used by permission of Doubleday, a division of Bantam Doubleday Dell Publishing Group, Inc.

Page 125: "Lord, I'm in trouble" form *Still Time to Sing* by Catharine Brandt. (Minneapolis: Augsburg Publishing House, 1980). Used by permission of Catharine Brandt.

Page 125: "Addiction. It's got hold of me, God" from *Plain Prayers in a Complicated World*. Reprinted by permission of Avery Brooke and available from Cowley Publications at 800/225-1534.

Page 126: "God of oneness, wholeness" from *Praying Our Goodbyes* by Joyce Rupp. Copyright © 1983 Ave Maria Press, Notre Dame, IN. Used by permission.

Page 126: "From moment to moment" by Teresa of Avila. (1515-1582).

Page 127: "Wake up little baby God," Source unknown.

Page 127: "O Love, no more sins!" by Catherine of Genoa. (c.1447-1510).

Page 128: "When I'm down and helpless," a Czech litany, Source unknown.

Page 129: "May the God of mercy who is well acquainted" from *Swallow's Nest: A Feminine Reading of the Psalms* by Marchiene Vroon Rienstra. Copyright © 1992 Wm. B. Eerdmans Publishing Co. Used by permission.

And I Will Give You Rest

Page 132: "You, who said, 'Come unto me'" from *I've Got to Talk to Somebody God* by Marjorie Holmes. Copyright © 1968, 1969 Marjorie Holmes Mighell. Used by permission of Doubleday, a division of Bantam Doubleday Dell Publishing Group, Inc.

Page 132: "I'm tired, Lord" by Saidie Patterson, England. Source unknown.

Page 133: "How is it, my God, that you have given" by Teresa of Avila, Spain (1515-1582).

Page 134: "We seek rest where there is no rest" from *Meditations with Julian of Norwich* by Brendan Doyle. Copyright © 1983 Bear & Co., Santa Fe NM. Used by permission.

Page 134: "Dear God, it is so hard for us" by Monica Furlong. Used by permission.

Page 135: "The Lord is here," by Michi Kawai of Japan for World Day at Prayer 1950. Copyright © 1949 United Council of Church Women. Used by permission.

Page 136: "How should I fear to die?" by Teresa Hooley. Source unknown.

Page 136: "God is not only fatherly" from *Meditations with Mechtild of Magdeburg* by Sue Woodruff. Copyright © 1982 Bear & Co., Santa Fe, NM. Used by permission.

Page 137: "I am alone in the dark" from *The House at Rest*. Copyright © 1984 Discalced Carmelite Nuns, Pewaukee, WI. Used by permission.